Animales del zoológico / Zoo Animals

LOS TUCANES
TOUCANS
AT THE ZOO

Seth Lynch

Traducido por / Translated by Esther Ortiz

Gareth Stevens
PUBLISHING

Please visit our website, www.garethstevens.com. For a free color catalog of all our high-quality books, call toll free 1-800-542-2595 or fax 1-877-542-2596.

Library of Congress Cataloging-in-Publication Data

Names: Lynch, Seth, author.
Title: Los tucanes / Toucans at the zoo / Seth Lynch.
Description: New York : Gareth Stevens Publishing, [2020] | Series: Animales del zoológico / Zoo animals | Includes index.
Identifiers: LCCN 2018039581| ISBN 9781538243671 (library bound)
Subjects: LCSH: Toucans–uvenile literature. | Zoo animals–Juvenile literature.
Classification: LCC QL696.P57 L96 2020 | DDC 598.7/2–dc23
LC record available at https://lccn.loc.gov/2018039581

First Edition

Published in 2020 by
Gareth Stevens Publishing
111 East 14th Street, Suite 349
New York, NY 10003

Translator: Esther Ortiz
Editor, English: Therese Shea
Designer: Katelyn E. Reynolds

Photo credits: Cover, p. 1 buteo/Shutterstock.com; p. 5 rainyclub/Shutterstock.com; p. 7 (top left) DDCoral/Shutterstock.com; p. 7 (top right) Mike Price/Shutterstock.com; p. 7 (bottom left) Eric Isselee/Shutterstock.com; p. 7 (bottom right) apple2499/Shutterstock.com; p. 9 Surkov Vladimir/Shutterstock.com; p. 11 DeLoyd Huenink/Shutterstock.com; p. 13 Rodrigo Friscione/Image Source/Getty Images; pp. 15, 24 (bill) jo Crebbin/Shutterstock.com; pp. 17, 24 (tongue) Brian Lasenby/Shutterstock.com; p. 19 julianufer/Shutterstock.com; p. 21 Tacio Philip Sansonovski/Shutterstock.com; p. 23 Art Montes De Oca/Photographer's Choice/Getty Images.

Printed in the United States of America

CPSIA compliance information: Batch #CS19GS: For further information contact Gareth Stevens, New York, New York at 1-800-542-2595.

Contenido

Contents

Veo tucanes
en el zoológico.
¡Aprendo mucho!

....

I see toucans at the zoo.
I learn a lot!

Hay cerca de 35 tipos de tucanes.

There are about 35 kinds of toucans.

El más grande
es el tucán toco.

The biggest is
the toco toucan.

Los tucanes viven
en bosques tropicales.

....

Toucans live
in rain forests.

Viven en los agujeros de los árboles.

They live in tree holes.

Tienen un pico grande.

••••••••••••••••••••••••••••••

They have a big bill.

Tienen una lengua muy larga.

....

They have a long tongue.

Los tucanes comen fruta. También comen pequeños animales.

....

They eat fruits. They eat small animals.

¡Los tucanes son muy ruidosos!

They are loud!

Me gustan los tucanes
del zoológico.

I like toucans
at the zoo!

Palabras que debes aprender
Words to Know

(el) pico
bill

(la) lengua
tongue

Índice/Index